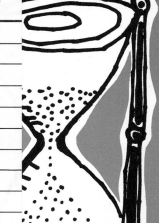

DATE DUE

APR 2 7 1989	
APR 1 5 1991	
APR 1 3 1992	
MAY 0 4 1994	
DEC 1 5 1995	
OCT 2 3 1996	
~~DEC 1 5 1997~~	
DEC 0 9 1997	
FEB 1 9 2001	

OTHER BOOKS IN THE SCIENCE PARADE SERIES

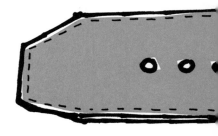

JUST A MINUTE

a book about time

by LEONORE KLEIN

Illustrated by LEONARD KESSLER

**A
SCIENCE
PARADE
BOOK**

HARVEY HOUSE, INC.
Publishers
Irvington-on-Hudson, N. Y.

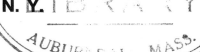

Is your mother like everybody's mother?

Does your mother say almost every night, "Hurry. Hurry. Scurry. Scurry. It's time for bed"?

And are you like every boy and every girl?

Do you say, "Just a second, Mother. I'll be ready in just a second"?

What is your second like?

Is it like every boy's second and every girl's second? Is it a very long second, especially at bedtime?

It probably is.

But a second is real. You can hear it on a watch.
Tick. Tick. Tick.

You can see it on a clock.
Quick, quick, quick goes the second hand.

What is a second, and what can you do in just a second?

You can clap your hands. You can wink your eye.

You can throw a ball. You can jump up high.

You can wiggle your toes and say, "Good-by" in a second.

Try it.

Are you like every other boy and every
girl?

When you and your mother are out for
a walk, and she meets a friend and starts to
talk, do you say, "Hurry, Mother. Hurry.
Please stop talking. Let's keep walking"?

And is your mother like everybody's mother? Does she say, "Just a minute. I'll stop talking in just a minute"?

What is your mother's minute like? Is it a very long minute? Does it seem like an hour?

It probably does.

But a minute is real, just like a second.
There are sixty seconds in a minute.
What can you do in just a minute?

ONE MINUTE

SIXTY SECONDS
IN ONE MINUTE

JIN-GLE BELLS, JIN-GLE BELLS, JIN-GLE ALL THE WAY!

You can hop and skip right down the block.

You can finish a small sized lollypop.

You can hit a ball and run and run—around the bases and home again.

You can sing a song. That doesn't take long.

Try "Jingle Bells."

There are sixty minutes in an hour, and so many seconds you can hardly count them. Do you know how many seconds there are in an hour? There are 3,600 seconds.

SIXTY MINUTES IN ONE HOUR … COUNT THEM!

It's hard to sit still and watch a clock for 3,600 seconds, for sixty minutes, for one long hour.

But there are all kinds of things that you can do in an hour's time.

You and your mother can bake a cake.

You can play a game of checkers. You can pitch a game of ball.

You can make a house of sand and surround it with a wall.

Or you can make a snowman. That's a lot of fun.

In 3,600 seconds, in sixty minutes, in one hour, you can easily finish one.

Some hours rush by in a minute. An hour of playing does that. But when you wait an hour for Dad to come home, it seems like a day, doesn't it?

Twenty-four hours make a day. Twelve
hours are for sleeping and twelve hours are
for play.

Do you sleep twelve hours? Sometimes?
Never? Always?

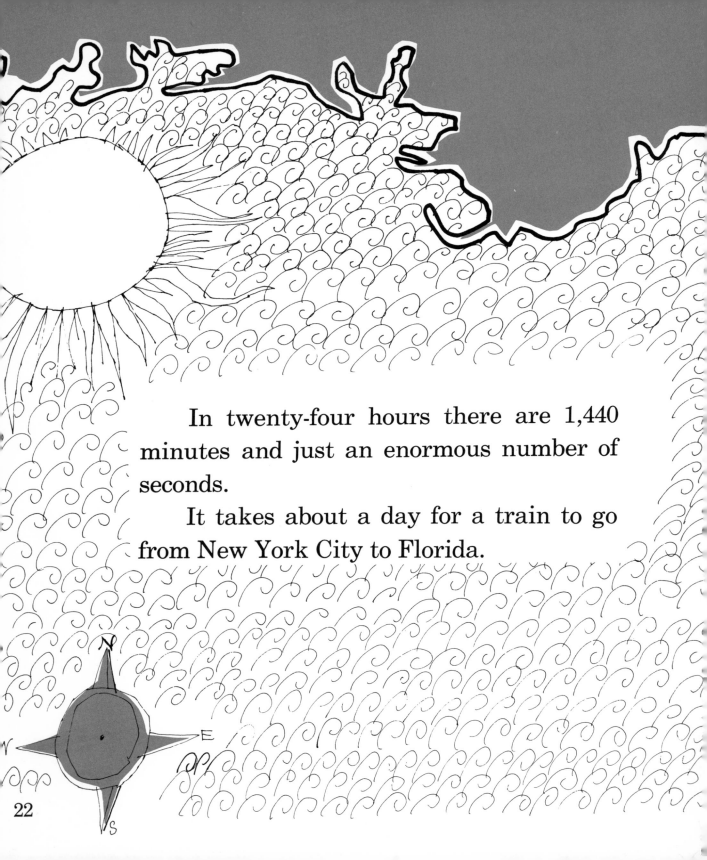

In twenty-four hours there are 1,440 minutes and just an enormous number of seconds.

It takes about a day for a train to go from New York City to Florida.

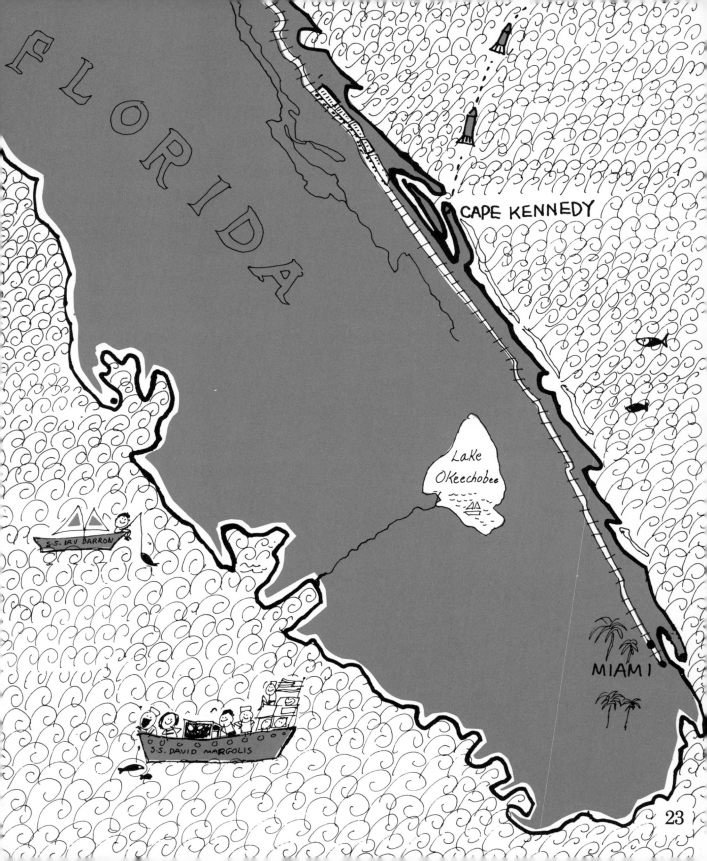

FLORIDA

CAPE KENNEDY

Lake Okeechobee

S.S. IRV BARRON

MIAMI

S.S. DAVID MARGOLIS

23

And about a day for a letter to go from from New York City to Washington.

A mother bird will lay an egg in just about a day.

And a lily bud will open up and then will die away—in twenty-four hours.

As for Daddy's face, in just one day it
will get all bristly.

"No, Daddy," you'll say. "Until you
shave, you just can't kiss me."

Most fathers shave every day.

There are so many things that you can do in twenty-four hours. You can skate, play house, and ride a bike, paint, cut out dolls, and model with clay, sleep and eat breakfast, lunch, and dinner—all in a day.

A day can sometimes seem like a year —especially the day before your birthday.

60 SECONDS IN A MINUTE

60 MINUTES IN AN HOUR

24 HOURS IN A DAY.........

MONDAY 5 TUESDAY 6 WEDNESDAY 7 THURSDAY 8

There are sixty seconds in a minute and sixty minutes in an hour. There are twenty-four hours in a day. What comes next? A week? That's so.

A week is longer than a second and
even longer than a minute. A week is longer
than a day. As a matter of fact, seven days
are in it: Monday, Tuesday, Wednesday,
Thursday, Friday, Saturday, Sunday. Lots
of things can happen in a week.

29

A tadpole swimming in the creek can change into a frog.

A ship can sail across the sea—from the United States to Italy.

Johnny can get a cold and then—he can get all better again—in a week.

Have you ever gone on a week's vacation? You have? To the beach? To a lake? To a farm?

Did you swim? Did you hike? Did you catch a fish?

Yes. Vacations for a week are fun, but
not such fun when they are done.

If you can wait about one hundred years, you'll probably reach Mars in a week.

And over one hundred years ago, it took a week just to go from Boston to New York City and back.

Weeks are very long, of course, but months are even longer.

There are about thirty-one days and hundreds of hours and millions of seconds in a month of ours. And, of course, about four weeks, too. An awful lot can happen to you in a month.

You can lose your two front teeth, and two new ones can grow in.

Your hair can get so long it can almost
reach your chin—in a month. Most people
need haircuts every month.

A duck egg can become a duckling.

A boy can plant a seed. The seed can grow into a radish, a flower, or a weed—in a month.

And a man can build a boat, and men can build a house in about thirty-one days —in about four weeks time.

But, in a year, oh, me, oh, my, when twelve whole months have all gone by, so much can happen!

Your head can grow so very much you'll need a brand-new hat.

Your baby sister can learn to walk.

Your kitten can become a cat.

Each year you move up one grade higher.

You usually get a brand-new teacher.

And, in a year, each boy or girl has
one special day. Can you guess what it is?
That's right.

A birthday. A HAPPY BIRTHDAY!
Every year.

A second.

A minute.

An hour.

A day.

A week.

A month.

A year.

Each one of these is very different. But, still, in one way, they're the same.

They measure time. They tell us when, how long, how short, how fast, how slow, how early, and how late.

And they go on and on and on. They just don't wait.

And now—let's hear what you can do
In a year,
In a month,
In a week,
In a day,
In an hour,
In a minute,
In a second.

Date Due